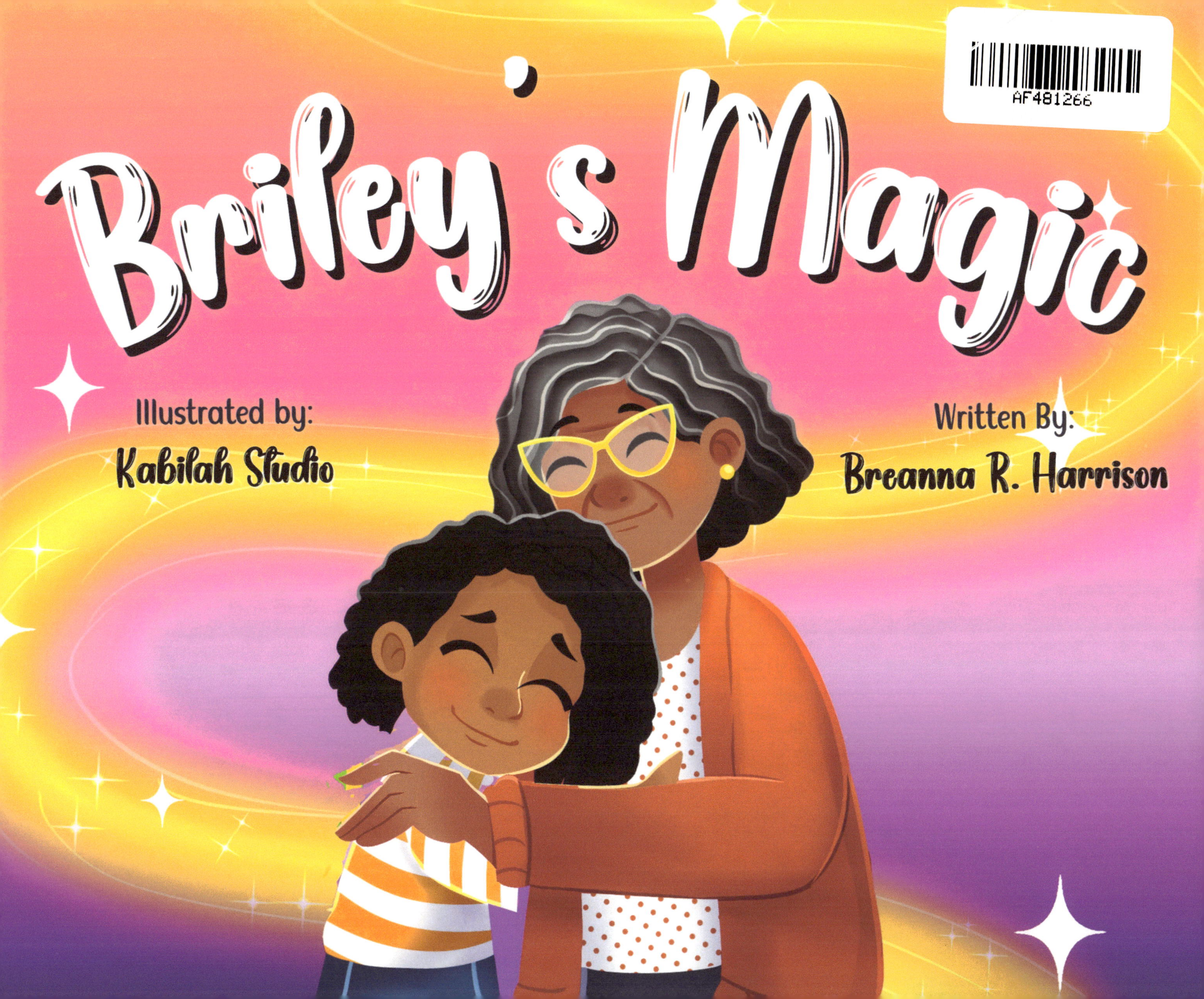
Briley's Magic
Illustrated by:
Kabilah Studio
Written By:
Breanna R. Harrison
AF481266

This book is dedicated to my great-grandmother, Varibess (BeBe). Thank you for raising me to be the woman I am today. You are a light in my life, always.
 -Love Bre

Hello! My name is Briley and I am here to say,
That sometimes my life is happy and sometimes it is just okay.

I feel happy when I am reading and playing with my friends.

But sometimes, I get really sad and have negative thoughts in my head.

Sometimes I cry and begin to feel down,
about the way I look, the way I talk, and sometimes the way I sound.

Kids at school say these things to me and it makes me cry.

But my grandma tells me to not pay attention to them and hold my head high.

My grandma is my best friend because we spend time with one another.
We bake sweets, go to church, and always sing together.

She is the best person I know and I love her very much.
From the way she dresses, her bright smile, and her warms hugs that bring me luck.

So when I am feeling sad, and want to curl up in my bed,

she comes, tells me to listen up, and this is what she says:

I am Special!

My Grandma says I am Special and one of a kind. She even wanted to name me Precious, because that's what I am in her mind.

I am Beautiful!

My Grandma says I am Beautiful with a great big smile. My hair is thick, my skin is brown, and it makes her day worthwhile.

I am Smart!

My Grandma says I am Smart and I never give up on anything.
No matter how hard the task, I accomplish everything.

I am Blessed!

My Grandma says I am Blessed and a gift from heaven above.
She is always praying and giving thanks that I am here to show her love.

I am Funny!

My Grandma says I am Funny in my own quirky way.
She is always smiling and laughing at the hilarious things I say.

I am Proud of Me!

My Grandma is the smartest person in the world, that I know for sure.
So if she says I am all these great things, it must definitely be true.

I have Power!

Now whenever I get sad and feeling a little sour
I remember what my grandma says and that gives
me POWER.

I am Magical!

My grandma's words are like Magic. She makes me feel better in every way.
I listen to what she says about me and I remind myself everyday.

I am Confident!

So whenever you feel down, go ask your favorite person what makes you special and how much you are a blessing.

I am Wonderful!

Listen to what they say and remember it in your heart,
so you can remind yourself of those things when you both are apart.

What makes you special?

What do you love about
yourself?

Thank you for reading
Briley's Magic

Check out my other books and more at
www.mvpbooks.org

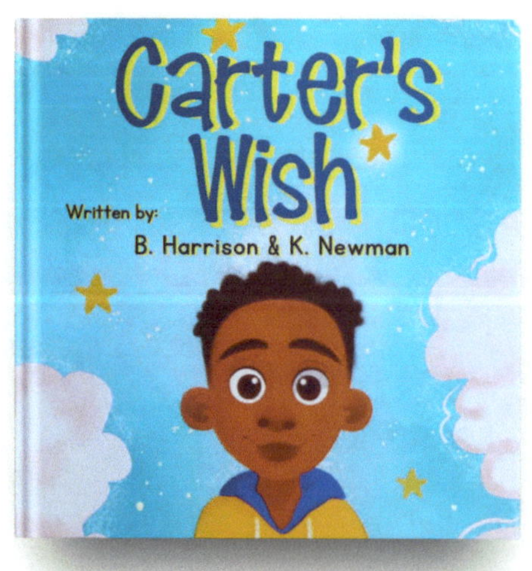

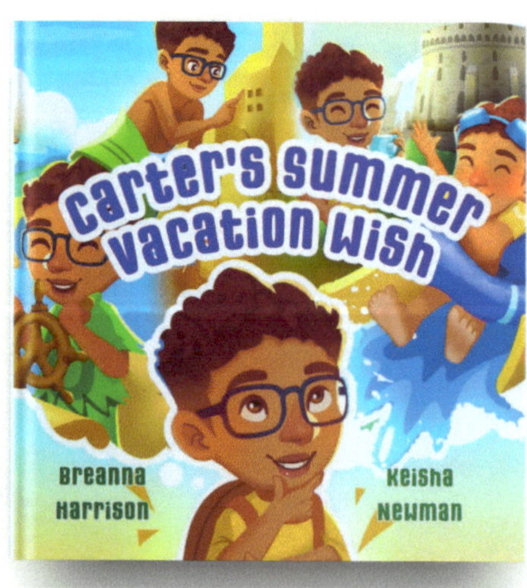

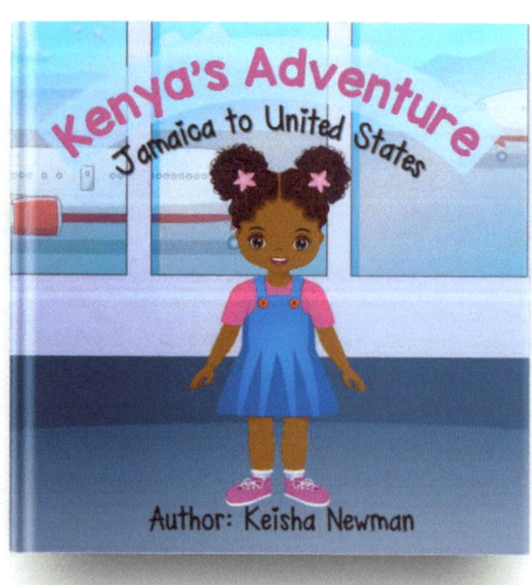

About the Author:
Breanna R. Harrison

I am a professional school counselor and a children's book author! When the daily hustle and bustle gets too much, I escape into the world of books and let my imagination run wild. I'm on a mission to bring the wildest stories to life through my children's books.

But wait, there's more! My great grandmother was my number one supporter and shaped who I am today. She had a special kind of magic that inspired me, and I want to share that enchantment with the world. So, I wrote a story straight from my heart about the bond we shared, hoping it'll touch others just like it touched me.

www.ingramcontent.com/pod-product-compliance
Lightning Source LLC
Chambersburg PA
CBHW041033120726

48005CB00004B/792